Songs of Genesee

POEMS

Pamela Livingston

CEREUS BOOKS 2018

SONGS OF GENESEE © 2018 BY CEREUS BOOKS

The cover image was made with vegetable prints of potato and apple.
The author created the artwork using Chinese ink and brush.

ISBN 978-0-9989988-0-0

to my fire father
  from his water daughter

Songs of Genesee

Come, architects
I seek a structure
based on harmony
not linear, not chronology
but arched prettily, like a
bower, festooned with flowers
where tensions soften to the
ground... poetry as medicine
energy of sound

At the princess fountain of the
    Incas, water still flows
        sweet to drink—
turned off and on by the
    stroke of a finger
gentle across smooth lip of stone—
so deep and discreet
    is this love between
    humans and water.

Thank you, grandmother Sun
and father Moon,
  gold in the water
    fire in the water—
Straight into the
  heart of love—
  mother's milk
  nectar, dew
    radiance
  from above
  down to you

and me too

Everywhere, in the bus, the hotel
the airport—women are talking
about Water. Our subject, our life...
how it is labelled and sold, traded
for gold, piped and spoiled, wasted
and stored—and mostly
how it flows
      so near to our hearts
         and universal soul,
            solvent and solution,
      we speak of it with
      penetrating love.

You know how the ladybug's wings
begin to part—and, slightly parted,
start to quiver before it flies?
   That's how it feels—a clinging
of uncertainty, to thrill.
   A holding to the earth
so springing forth can be
            the greater still.
   I am not dying, yet new I seem to be.
I now must tune my instrument differently—
   muscles unused grow bright
for things they don't yet know....
     The vision is alive
and has been seen—to let go
    is all that remains.
Rattle the seeds! prepare for flight.
    Quiver
       as you please

Many men want to control
    the women's powers
        control the waters
indulge obsessions—their engines
rumble constantly, cutting lawns
cutting trees—or dreaming of Nothing
lost in the rumble, out of control
    so they want to control others,
        Wasting gasoline.
        And then again,
any moment
    a tree might breathe on them
        its last breath—as it is felled.
And the men wake up holy
(it happened to a man I know,
    a *petrolero*)

Anger prodded me
   and poems came out
Fear was sent
and pain to temper me
   another skin shed
and muscles tremble
with the unknown—
   the opening
of the mysterious female
     is also called
   the valley spirit
   undying,
root of heaven and earth

These are the days of weeding and pruning
of getting stung and pricked
Days of bleeding and singing, glorious days
of nettles and thistles, roses and thorns
Days of cleaning, preparing—feeling, releasing
old wounds healing
Days of abundance, berries and plums
beans and tomatoes
Days of the brightest flowers of all
These are the days
of tasting, preparing—days of sharing
Autumn is coming
   Winter is coming
These are the blessing days
      with long rosy
         golden rays
           of the sun.

I told my parents, when I grow up
I'm going to live in a cave or a tree.
I have felt these things in me,
have climbed and dug bravely.
The earth was protector to me,
the trees were my shelter
The river was my king, and
the mother, its valley—
The Valley Spirit—boundless giving,
endless giving, life-giving—
beautiful river valley—
                Genesee
I thank thee, for your gifts
of crystal clarity.
Riverine I'll always be, as were
my parents'
families
before me.

yes, said the helicopter pilot, river is life
        river is community,
               all over the world.

It sometimes felt I got
too full of secrets
        to be well—
witholding common goods,
as life in a rumbling cloud
       stifling upon a hill.

              Let it rain!

how else can we bring in
anything new?
I invite my irrepressible self
to dissolve all conflict from within
with the kindness that is there;
a major battle has begun,
enterprise of many—
many sages through the ages,
many who have won,
discovering another way
not domination.
I wage this war of peace
with all nations, with wisdom
new and ancient,
       and all of nature
to understand the way.

SOLIDAGO

...there's Goldenrod's face
in the shadow it makes—
tall lady with a fine expression
of contentment and strength—
she bows down in the wind,
stands up again proud
to enjoy her season finally come—
    green lips and golden hair
  (cheerful Aster is her friend.)
Patient and quiet were her leaves
silent her stem,
  as it slowly grew,
unnoticed until she bloomed.

    I am a player
in the overthrow of a
tyrannical system.
    We gather like sticks
circling as in a nest, to birth the new.
I freely declare and honor my
indigenous roots, branches and leaves,
needing no legitimacy from any tribe,
decree, or degree of approval
any more than a blade of grass
        or puff of wind.

I have a shell in an upstairs room
    which has the sea sound
    and I forget to listen—
Waves of breath lap at my shore
    telling me who I am—

(I can tell I have grown, because
when a jungle girl puts my hair
in braids, I don't pull it
out straightaway like I did
in my youth.
Now I can receive —
it doesn't impinge upon
my freedom,
as I used to think.)

Gone are the honey-solemn songs
bent rods and flutes of river cane—
    Done we are, with dead offerings
        while the thirst and the
            water remain.
I am in the place of seeing, now—
    putting on my new grey shoes
for walking in the mist invisibly
    and stepping where I choose—
    Ah bored country!
Your giant walks again
        sure-footed, broad and feeling
    to sweep away debris,
let acheing long-held under skin
evaporate as rain—
a forgotten fluidity returns to me.
I am in the place of seeing now,
    for here on this battlefield, all
must labor, see themselves, and fall—
All must labor, aye, in joy
        Joy, all

Green grasses share their dances
   and reeds their song and mattress—
there will be a lively rest; earth
dreams anew, her vision blessed
in you—braided one, two, three
true strands.

> I go to the place of
>   my father — to pay
> homage to the ten comings
>   and the five goings.
> We bow down to each other
>   constantly —
> this is the way it should be,
>   like a fountain
>   we become.

When I went to the bathroom, moonlight
was splashed upon the floor like spilt blood —
I stepped in it. What is this connection between
    blood and the moon? Startling,
        can be the light of the moon.
I wanted to sleep but couldn't,
and night soon turned to day. I wanted to turn things around.
I didn't like how people were talking
about the end of the world, as if it was okay —
meanwhile such a force of nature and of love was at work
constantly, keeping the delicate balance —
                or is it play?
Words too trite don't penetrate.
    I wanted to talk to children
in a way they would understand, and they
showed me, with whole body
    and we laughed
a different laugh, not the silly echo
of cynical people who are sad about the world,
but laughter so free its ripples could change the world
    I think, bring it into harmony.
And the old people too, they laughed — it was
    medicine to my bones
    and startling, too
        like the bright moonlight.

A bird flew by,
a simple bird, in the barren sky
I watched it fly

The rain came down,
a softly dying delicate sound
To feed the ground.

My grandpa died.
A happy life, but still
I cried.

A bird flew by….

UNDERWORLD

I don't think I can perceive
all my gifts and blessings
without accepting
        everything as love.
Time proves me wrong
when I reject narrowly and judge
the exploits and pitfalls
of a former self. This
  is the exquisition, it's safe
to grow and bloom
and never too late, to see perfection
        and not hate.

Something free and equitable
we're bottling up, in some wrong name
    which asks of us too much.
      Love cracks me open
        by my own pain.

WISH

You should not bruise it with your hope,
don't blow too hard your hope upon it,
something that you wish. Let it go
like the praying mantis which flew
from the balcony with white wings
I didn't know it had,
over the dark palm tree gardens.
I had set it free,
   yet its freedom surprised me.
Do not bruise it with your doubt, it could be
creation, or birth beyond imagining,
too tender, too specifically alive
to bear the weight of your desire—
let it be an opening, your heart.

        A child stood there by the road
tending a flock of sheep. A tiny child,
desire like that—guarding your health,
your life, standing by.

(Then why do I feel sad and alone up on
this hill? A taster, a feeler of wind and
raindrops on my skin. A storm blows in.
It's late summer now. I have too much
of everything.)

To break away from oppression
is creative, like breaking through
   an egg from within.
If it is broken from outside — well
      that might be death not life.
   If someone assumes what color
I will be, or what shape, they are wrong.
By my Nature, must I destroy you?
Can I?   In my vulnerability I
will not let you destroy me —
   I will use the force of your
      opposition to engage my soul
         and body in its opening.

FROG KING

Stormy and wonderful night—
I love the excitement of you,
your thunder and light
and fresh water pouring from the sky!
You are my lover tonight, my teacher
and friend.
The sound of rain is my blessing,
your wind a wild caress.
The frog in his element came! And then he left.
Yes it's a wonderful night on the Amazon riverbank,
bamboo waving like a hurricane,
in the wetness, soft wetness,
   of a half-moon honeymoon—
for you I dress, dear storm, for you
inspire me to be myself again.
Do I dare say romantic? To the end—
opening as only a flower can,
washed by a storm, entered by a storm
loved by a storm.

Chapter 2 — Gradual Development
                              (emerging from the chrysalis)
Inner tranquility protects against
rash and sudden moves
which would tear at the developing wings...
   weakness
is here for a reason.
No-one will invade the sacred space of my development.
   I will emerge when I am ready.
Everything has a purpose, and within this space it becomes
                  clear.
In the simplest way possible,

                        I emerge.

Law of life — isn't it funny to think
that lies — in their extreme (as in govt.
and business corruption) might naturally —
and do — give birth to truth?
As yang turns to yin at its fullness
and yin to yang —
and that sickness might
lead to health?
      I cannot (will not) be
      tamed.

    signed,
        the Tiger

Solitude with my allied spirits
in this cave as in the
dark-night-jungle-*dieta*-net,
to birth the songs and gospel of a new soul
(imagined, real) I have not met yet.
    Nature spirits,
        mermaids,
    tree-top toad goblins,
        pink dolphins,
           manatees,
condors, electric eels—
   all of us are part of this—
in harmony? It's up to me.
I am not afraid of giving birth.

The turning—
    There is the sense of
something hidden in our periphery,
lost to time and space
trembling to be noticed—it will
not jump into my face until
I turn there

As the steward of my life —
   it can't be hurried, or shorn
by outsiders who haven't seen
   or understood what kind of plant
or animal or mineral am I —
Much work to do inside!
   In the pale grey morning
I swam circling in the center
      of a quiet pond.
Loving the water, its heavenly embrace
like cool velvet on my nakedness
    took away my fear.
Like a small whirlpool I knew I could trust
the emerging words, their intention
      to form a whole
  book like a deep pond.
Succession of thought ripples
   intersecting into the
      eventuality of fact:
     it's the state of affairs
    order of the day
   the world
   destiny.

THE OLD MERMAID

Adventure-giver, Quiverer — at twilight
she sits on a giant lily-pad,
    stars on her nipples; the old mermaid
is true to her sagging breasts. Pathetic,
they call her — but she is my flower,
mother of the lake.
        Disasters under her,   distant thunder...
           her realm is innocence
                and undying love.

Dear women and men,
    I draw upon your strength.
     I am your affirmation,
aligned with the soul, the collective
  and my own.
We will not project enmity
    where there is love
or find comfort in falsity
when the sun shines its truth
and the moon shines hers....
So much beauty, limitless in this world
    so much music not yet heard—
drifting for a moment, for old time's sake—
    a journey with a purpose
      I must now make.

GEOMETRY

Through the vesica of my eye, the
triangle temple of your calf and thighs—
a pool of gold water, where our fingers play
    where they swim, make love,
    dance to the sun, and we laugh
    like gods, lying on the rock
        on holiday.

The world makes you
       forget
but there's nothing
that matters quite so much
   as your mother's touch.

A shard, a shred, her shawl — won't do,
      is not enough.
It's her living hand that has the stuff —
the strength of lullabies, with fire inside
and in her eyes — all waters of the world
      unite.

A sadness spreads.
   I see it through.
Like a bad spell, it took me too.
I could not remember
   but now I do, and there's
nothing quite so
   beautiful.

At first it was a whiff of hope
Then empty as a bone
A breath blew through, and sounded it
I knew it was my own—

And in the night it came again
and whispered by my bed—
(we wish that you would not forget)
obey the golden voice, it said.

Come, architects —
    I seek a structure
  based on harmony
not linear   not chronology
      but arched prettily
    like a bower
  festooned with flowers,
  where tensions soften
    to the ground.
    Poetry as medicine,
      energy of sound...
have you seen the rattle doctor?
    He visits here sometimes —
    so pleasing is his work, so fine...

the best can't go in words, anyway —
    the Swamp   the Pond
      the Pretty Place,
  the Cliff —
  the Cliff where the sweet black birch grew,
    whose twigs we chewed,
      and out came —
        songs.

So now in this brazen autumn
   even in which some friends have died,
my energy too must go back to the roots
   like the dandelion and burdock.
How dark it seems—
      how deep!
        how easy to forget
   the way is open to return...
   but first—take, eat—
and praise the falling leaves around me golden—
   I will play my oldest ukulele,
   the one my grandmother played as a girl
   and this is roots music,
      my own.

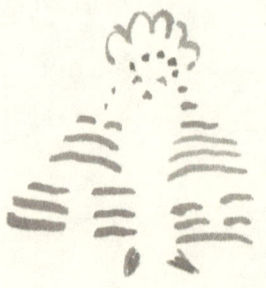

Apu, they call
the pointed mountain,
looking up, to where it
points: a condor flies
through clouds like seas
     and in the mist
the mountain weeps
dissolving hardness into
heart of flesh, and rivers
into seas.

I AM AMERICA, BLOOMING
(TEXAS, 1972)

America is dying, and is being born.
Dreams of people are lying around
shattered and torn, on the ground.
But our tears are the rain—sweet rain!
And up out of the pain
  love grows,
    like an ear of Corn

I see the Sun
    under a cloud
ready to set—
    shining out loud
      O beauty
my heart is a rose
    which,
        once it is open
cannot ever close.

Every last blooming flower
wears its own shimmering
insect, as the sweet and bitter
season draws to an end,
fulfilled.

Every word seems to have its opposite
(beginning in the thesaurus with
Existence/Nonexistence). Every meaning
has its converse and opposing force,
which gives to language a kind of power
to play a part in the drama.
    This does not diminish the truth
beyond expression, beyond
male and female or all the differences
on which we can blame our own
confusion.
Water in the river's made more lively
by currents warm and cool
which mingle but never entirely
mix.
So it is to the
spirit of all that I appeal for help in this
communication, against all odds, trusting
in the you in me, the me in you.

I barely know where to start,
with poetry—
    it startles and surprises me.
It wasn't planned to be a fruit
but shows its face now as my root
   and here I must obey.
Dwelling awhile in deep earth thought.
    I might just stay

    and find again
   a core of molten joy.
You wish me to deny
the magic of my life,
forsaking—for your fear—
all that I know and love?
You cannot snuff me out.
Signed,
        the Bear

THE MOUNDBUILDER

Once, ages ago, a sweet goddess-like maid
    lived in a wood in a glade of green moss.
At each dawn and each dusk she would cross
    her glade of soft moss,
to a hill she had made, of all the beautiful things
    she found in the wood.
The toadstools and stars, the flowers,
        the stones —
all were contained in that fast-growing
    mound.
The longer she lived, the more that she found.
And then when she died, the deep scars
    of her death were left
        in the wood,
    and the beauty she made
    was where it had stood.

The cave of my heart says 'Beware',
        be aware, not afraid —
            (there's a bear in there...)
we're hurtling towards the darkest day,
we'll come through it like the Sun
having shed unnecessaries, and still shedding
one by one — the dark reveals
what has begun — a New Year glimmers,
        kind, and fun.
Goodbye, unnecessary thoughts and worries
and I thank you for your troubles —
        (you are neutralized.)

I too was once in jail — glad to be released
and yet the memory remains,
of affection for a place
    where one felt peace.
la Muerte they call me,
from the other cell
where they play *loteria* and up comes the skull —
death and life were one — the snake tasted its tail,
it was sweet like corn, wild as fireworks,
gentle as oleander and salt mist from the sea

  which wafted through the bars to comfort me
on the worn stone floor I saw
the Earth was filled with light, circled by a rainbow
and ringed with trees. I did it in embroidery
with colored threads the jailers brought,
so I would not forget, so I would one day remember
my old jail

    and re-visit the freedom I felt there,
  and the place itself.

Rhythms stayed in me from the
land of milk and honey—
nourishment brings freedom—
    forget your worries
    forget your self!
my freedom rendered me
    totally absorbed.

MEADOW AT NIGHT

The cows were quiet once the stars came.
They did not sleep.
To and fro they turned their big black heads
   while sweet vapors curled like smoke
       from their mouths.
They looked at each other silently,
     then turned to the silvery moon-grass
       at their feet
to sniff and eat.
They never saw the stars but on their
       backs
   they felt them, tingling
and they swished their tails
over the bones.

The sun's a wastrel,
     the moon is dark.
A cold wind blows through
   the cave of my heart
which cannot fathom
   warm necessity — reality
calls but where's the strength
to see?
   Maybe in sleep 'twill be
restored, in sleep and dreaming
by its own light
awaken,
       find me O Sun!
pine needles strewn
this solstice eve,
     before the fire....
Do we dare
   to show angelic tendencies
     unique and rare?

    Big Indian Rock
on the first day of winter
I taste the snow fallen on you,
water crystals
   absorb your memory   your power
bold and complex piece of earth wisdom.
On you I was a virgin dreaming
     child climbing   maiden seeing
to other rocks like you I've been, and called them
Mother—but you are mine, to whom my thread
is tied.

Simple I am, Genesee —
a complicated story is my web
rape   kidnapping   control
a curse or two of jealous rage
have touched my body at a tender age
and my soul.
So new I'm old-fashioned,
so old I'm like a child —
What is that lubrication of free thought —
or is it Love, that lets the spider navigate
its web, not stuck like prey,
   but to live instead? Oil on the feet they say
Wrap up the pain — eat, regurgitate
       renew the web.
A banner's woven into mine
since olden times —
It's waving in the breeze,
truth without fear, it says
  Verite Sans Peur

Persevere, says my spirit mother,
I have high hopes for you, who dare
       to bloom....
    My art dispersed in all directions
    like mist, coming to rest in the cold
shade of trees. Forest of the hidden valley.
Many years pass.
       Here I am still
   reconsidering my position
   wanting new expression
     here to give birth
can't you feel my suffering?

A Chrysalis needs
the warmth of the sun
    to shine into its pallor,
and quicken the gathering stillness.
I have a flickering candle,
    ray of hope, to start.
Morning will follow,
    and the Spring

Fire, Fire
   fire of desire—
come fan the flames
   of mine! By your will come dance
with water, by mine I will give birth
      to sons and daughters
   currents warm and cool—
O milky waves of the river!
Take us to a jungle pool
   where there floats a moon;
and
risen atop the trees, she fans down
    her glinting ecstasy—
       old holy songs I sang,
    the ones I'd hid and shunned.
Now it's clear they're not just mine,
   the fire of soul is one.

The snake swung down — a half moon hung
    shining in black branches — the night
    was warm and still — content.
I was delirious from smiling so wide;
    my jaw clunked from the inside —
        I could feel myself transforming,
    and I breathed this knowing in
        all the way down to my roots
        so I wouldn't forget,
        so the change would continue
                even while I slept.

I dreamt of a man called Po-Po, intellectual,
    distinguished, tall—
        quiet like my father, accomplished I was sure...
in what, I didn't know or can't remember, I had more
        fun with Bobo, a fool like me, the night before.
We wallowed in a cove with friends, a paradise with waves,
    with dolphins and no dangers
        in sandy-bottomed swells—
the cove was fringed with oaks, and olive trees,
    it might have been Capri, in ancient days.

   I dreamed of a sphere, living and precious,
of infinite softness, wrapped in cashmere —
loosely followed and protected and served,
as a cloud of bees accompanying their queen
on a journey....
   What is that dear sphere of earth, of womb-life,
all possibility
which frightens those who wish to have a grasp
on the world?
It's kin to our own awakening heart, a source
orgasmic beyond belief, and worthy of love
because it brings forth more....

the earth's my muse and mother,
I look no further — why should I?
   her milk is on my breath.

Little starship in the clearing
let the moon shine down on thee —
All around the wind is howling,
 Darkness only seems to be....
Up above, the stars are twinkling
and like a thousand eyes they see —
 your home is truth and love,
to me
    O children of the galaxy —
Little starship in the clearing
let the moon shine down on thee
All around, the wind is howling —
 Darkness only seems to be.

NEW BEGINNINGS

I said it would be
   completion. My friend
thought I meant 'the end'.
No, I said — a new beginning
   from root-fed assimilation
      it is born...but if we don't glimpse it
it is gone. So, spread wings in the dawn,
   dry your wings and fly.
       This is how I feel about moving:
in terms of adventure I'm like
   a full card — must concentrate and empty,
allow the creativity; the poetry is me
and the hills surround me, speaking softly
   high moist valley, in winter filled with snow
      in the snow we burrow, home for now.
Much to do, contemplation — new beginnings.

   Dirty and ripe
      is the root.
   I wash my face.

   Drank a dewdrop
   at my father's grave.

no-one talks about that God, the one
who responds to the heart's desire, who
knows, as if he lives there…
it makes you wonder — this beauty,
the unfolding — is it my imagination?
Who speaks about this God? I notice
how sweetly life is given, in every detail
prescribed — like corn, like mother's milk.
The gods people talk about are cruel gods
of finance and commerce and war, of
strange religions, health insurance industry
gods of sickness and fear. Better to make
something up, about a God of Goodness
(like that tree-top toad goblin who
protects weary travelers on their way)
and take pleasure in the thought, if
you haven't felt it, or have forgotten it,
        yourself.

In the end of human history
there is mystery—
   it always suffers us to
awaken, and pre-history
   was the same, I saw
in my mother's nakedness—
     we're
   the vessels that carry it.
   the mystery of love
is required
for any human life
   to go on
      beyond
   the end of history

my mother ever fertile
  (with your high hopes)
    protect me in my
  opening
  You — who dared
  me to bloom

SNAKE

I went to the city for pleasure,
                      and in shame
I went in deep where no-one knew my name
        and in the darkest part
            I made a nest
where I was free to do what I liked best

There I was queen, no dutiful princess
No mother there who had monopoly
        on art and sex
The door had a great strong lock;
        I had the key.
I opened it and closed it many times,
        not just for me.

The bed I built myself — it was narrow
        and small
I shared it generously, but not with all

A candle flickered on the wall.
        The shadows danced.
The ancient toilet played a waterfall
        for my romance

And in the next room I made a
        dining table
from a barnacle-covered giant spool
        of telephone cable.
The floor was painted blue, just
        like the sea,
and there, in my seashell temple
        I nurtured me.

In the third room I played music
    and I danced
and painted all night long until I tranced.

A skin was coming off, just like a
    snake
the more it shed the more I felt
    awake

Outside there were few trees,
    no grass at all
Smells of excrement and alcohol

And when I finally emerged newborn
    from my nest
I left that city,
    gratefully
        and blessed.

    I shake my shaggy behind,
       black bear's
      thick fur
walks into the forest
in my room, where the claws
          are hung on the wall,
       feathers from a lampshade —
    the rug, the bed,
         the chair…here I sit down

                (the Bear)

trust your sympathies, trust
in your own fragrant
possibilities.

Celebrate
   all good things, to sustain
the language of good things—
symbols lose their meaning
words become myth,
reality only virtual? In my lifetime
this is happening—where are
the adventurers?
Where are the pigs and chickens
raised and ticked by loving children?
Gone.
The rulers have made factory farms,
toxic chemicals, bombs and arms—
Who do you think you are?
     King of the Casbah?
Punks, stupids, nerds, freaks, cowards
   pious, killer, geeks—human being—
     I am all of these—
Celebrate all good things,
     to remember the Language
of good things,
which dissolves again wordless, into
   feeling.

A frozen spider creeps
        across the page,
he is the seer, he is the sage
bringing sparkling tidings of
        new life,
          of a new age.
He creeps through the fog of my breath
  in candle-light.
He creeps into the shadow of
        his death, in this
     cold dark jungle
       of night.

To integrate self-knowledge
with the artist's soul—
To generate something new
from what is old ? We are not old
    who dare to do this—
  a small ascent, and graceful-o
  the subtle union of arpeggio—
A heaven-sent obedience I hold
  like fruit in hand, half-eaten.

Standing in a torrent
    I fill these cups
one by one
while the force
nearly knocks me down,
saved only by my tears—
  vulnerability to the extreme
lends fortitude to the dream...

  to let go of suffering
  is a courageous act

Happyness, happiness,
I seem to have trouble
writing this word
as if I do not know it well...
   in the night, a voice
in my head said:
your disease is over you know.
yes I said,
it's time to be free.
I pick up my star in my right hand
   to throw back to the sky,
to make a bridge,
bridge of light for me to fly,
this very night
     I am alive.

Was it by negligence? obliviousness?
or was I spared by unnotice,
as if put in a basket in a reedy stream to drift
undetected, escaping conventionality—
        though marrying it for a time....
    Male butterflies captivate the female,
        enravish her with iridescent dust,
          a puff of scent-particles from the scales
          of his wings. Each related species, each
          individual with its own delicate scent—
perhaps I smelled my children...do we
smell our future, pick up the scent of the
right path, where we need to move and learn?
This does not in itself assure safety.
    Your own smell, though, can save your life—
    when attacked by a snake, you hurl your shirt
        in its path, distracting it.

You must go at once
    into your chamber
        to divine your destiny—
    meet and make love with it,
with devotion, never stopping
day and night, and be prepared to
               recognize....

CANYON

The canyon is the place
where the mountain opens
its legs and the stream comes out—
it is a place of birth, a dark place
a place where fear comes, and where
fear is let go, where it is transformed
into joy. It is the place where the bears
come from, where they go inside and
give birth. And it is the place of
dragonflies. It is the place where the
light rides on their wings in spirals
over the dark place. And where the
spiders have thrown their golden
strands from tree to tree. And this
place is a giving place, so, no matter
how deep and old, it is always new.
There is a sound coming from in there—
I can hear—like a wind but there is not
a breeze. Like a call, but it is not human
or animal. I hear it, but it has no name.

Blessings on the work
        bring in the light!
Candle in the morning,
        candle at night

There's no mountain I worship, no town
which looms like home — no person
  not even a river now.
There's that rock
I touched, but even that
sets it all in motion.
I might be a little whirlpool, *muyuna*...
    or is it the wind? more like
a small force,
    at once discriminating and detached —
      a voice?

I'm letting go of the past.

My chrysalis temple has cracks.
The light comes through, but it's a light
from no particular place, from everywhere
at once.
By letting go I have initiated this
strange new birth which is
      unidentified pure force —
  is this the center of indifference
through which all souls must pass?
A mere swirl? Or is it simply this,
the beginning of a new day.

The Word of God is a golden thread,
    woven into a perfect web—
the whole universe, shining bright!
as the Spider divine is letting out his line—
    so fine, so fine
He's spinning eternally, day and night

We are but drops of morning dew,
dancing drops of rainbow hue—
held by the word which passes through.

    We must know from where we come,
        quickly, quickly, one by one
for we're drying fast in the heat of the sun—

    but the love goes on....

And once we've met the maker of the web,
we'll serve him forever, as jewels on his thread.
    Joyfully, joyfully we'll dance 'round his web,
    to the glory of the music
        that plays in his head!

VER SACRUM

I had to have a ceremony
beauty being born, it's called
and in it, hearts are open wide,
hearts of gold
and I am deep in its embrace —
    tender and free…
        a voice comes up from
        an ancient stream
           and it is me.

EARLY SPRING

Along the ragged oaks
   along a ragged stream
      too young to hold its banks
        it kicks and leaps—
nothing is neat but all is clean
   the stage prepared by winter
      for spring's new dream
of lambs and puppies and violet leaves

Below the path
in the hollow of a rock—
     there's a magic spring
       which makes me stop.
Sunlight quivers on a soft green stone
   in the middle of a pool,
a mossy throne—a stool
to sit upon, but I did not,
because the fairy moss was delicate—

nearby, a silver waterfall turns gold
flashing through a leafless wood—
   no glittering city in the world
      compares!
or could ever tempt the fairies there.

There is a delicacy about the Spring here,
   which lasts and lasts.
The coolness moderates the blooming,
   so it doesn't come too fast.
Each moment of opening
   is a subtle treasure
   exquisite measure of time.

MOTHER'S DAY

The mother, my mother—
                these friends
remind me of different and beautiful
aspects of her. I am learning to receive
more of her unconditional strong living
energy in my heart—Mother Earth,
  Madre Naturaleza,
     Virgen de la Leche—Milky Way

At this time the warmth of the Sun
comes back to replenish you. A fresh
breeze blows. A bee buzzes and there is a
terribly wonderful exciting and powerful
feeling to the day—it is Mother's Day!

I put my feet
in the West Canada Creek
in the soft black silt
where the yellow iris blooms
by the black silt soft
where the deer swam across
and I saw from the bridge
the deer swimming slow
its fur looked red
and the sky was aglow
    All round its head
was the green of the edge
and the sky on the water
reflected it.
As it held its head
and it swam across, and the
leaves and the water
reflected it.

Sight comes out of mist
Flowers give hearing
Fire animates, and
Earth's gift is feeling.
Taste is granted by the air, and
Smell, the south wind brings.
Water gives us all a voice
   and it might sing — these are
the things that shape
the soul of man,
   it was thought long ago,
     and maybe it's so,
that we are indispensable,
to translate
   peace.

Peace — don't wish me peace
(said my step-grandmother to me)
Peace is boring, it's for cows in a field!
I want excitement!

   To travel in mists or rain, or
under stars and moon
     on jungle waterways
the fun will make you swoon.
The captain sees in the dark —
you leave your sorrows behind
the river has swallowed your fears,
the *madrugada* is kind —

those hours
before dawn, when so much goes on,
the fishing and the hunting....

Methinks I like the primal air
    of everyday adventures,
which lead me where
      they might continue.
I will not censor their
    effect on me—
responsible I am for all I feel,
and learning makes me whole.

BLUEBERRIES

I go wild in the blueberry patch,
first time picking in a year,
pawing like a bear, I forget—
which basket am I filling?
Twin baskets, which will fill first?
The belly, or the bucket getting heavy?
I sink to the ground
as the light shifts,
showing me berries hidden in blue shadows—
the sweet, the sweeter—the sweetest
is life itself, we learned long ago....
I forget my mouth.
My body becomes one blue belly, round
blue berry—tasting has turned to being.
I lost track of time long ago, now that
      the sweetness is mine.
I sink to my knees in a kind of greed,
    or is it response to holy need, to sweeten
      for the coming season, the bitter
        winter's brooding...?

Colorful — Overeaten
I am a fat cat,
wasted on the fruits of summer
Stretching out — though
I have to say I'm grateful for
all that gets to stretch and grow
and to feel the pleasure of it —
    maybe later, I
will get to feel another, the pleasure
of coming back to focus
  into the depths of myself, into
the night I go, to crouch
crouching and ready to spring!
    But first — feeling
      the warm/cool center of things.

The last Incan Emperor
    Atahuallpa
trembled in his prison,
when the conquerors
cruel betrayal chilled him, and he
pulled around his shoulders a cloak,
velvety and warm,
made of the skins of bats
    on his last night.
  Ransom of gold and silver
rooms filled high, could not
    save him from a lie.
Tears of the Sun, fecund Moon
crushed into fagots, melted to doom
the grand and glittering empire
                of Peru.

My love is a nocturnal hunter
gliding into the darkness
   of a flooded forest—my love
is a leaf-roofed house with no walls
which falls now,
back to jungle, to earth.

This is how the revolution will look.

The old worn skin's grown dull, inhibiting.
The snake can't see well—'spectacles', it's called—
this condition nearing the change—
the snake's more apt to strike out blind, defensive
like participants in an outworn system.
The jungle house falls down. Snake sheds its skin,
slithers freshly away.
The river morphs, leaving villages behind—
    whole civilizations abandoned
as it changes course,
obeying the laws of nature,
law of life—all is transmutable
not a pebble to be found
    stories wrap around the changes...
    filaments of light—show me my path!
    Where do I help, thus thrive?
Not die, not drag down in lies
like the sterile pornography of
    a false abundance

FIELD DAY

Kite field, Judy's field, zig-zag field—
>I've named a few—

Field day—the word comes to my mind today,
>must enter the field and play.

What field? Field of Wildflowers? Of Daisies?
Sunflowers? Or of Corn?
>The one in which I am most vast and humble
>all one, and all alone.
>>Caw Caw! go the crows

Empty or fallow, or full of hay,
>>I pluck a grass wand
>>on the pitch where I play

Milky dove,
        teach us love
Your two eggs in the nest
nursed by parents, both
are blessed with milk in breast—
Coo Coo O tender brood,
   here is your food.

Life — so fragile
Life, with its own protection
'I just think about God all the time',
said the man on the riverboat.
'So far, it's worked out fine.'

When a bird trills its song, the surface
   of the water trembles,
tiny ripples form
   here within a flooded forest
water is a membrane blown upon,
    reflecting sound as well as light
        in the otherwise-gloomy
        hunting ground.
    Farther out, the milky currents swirl—
   humid trees everywhere,
mosquitos blown here and there, by rain
when it comes
   and when it goes—the wind it makes.

    Do you have a totem? I asked the
   handsome hunter…
you know, a favorite animal?…
Mis hijos, (my children)
he said,
   *'Mis hijos son mis animales
     preferidos.'*

He laid some giant leaves upon a fallen tree,
a place for us to sit down safely, above the stinging
ants and centipedes
which crawl in wetted earth and rotted leaves
as rivulets roll down the trees
upon the gurgling ground; he whistled and he
sang to me the jungle sound. And soon the dusk
it echoed us, with chanting characters behind,
frog choruses and night-jar—
            fireflies turned high

SELF-CARE

Is it possible to draw vitality
from the roots of memory and forgetting,
so the energy which allowed me
to climb trees, and to hear
   wise words
         how not to fall
   might be renewed in me, to
grow and to raise a curtain,
   a hullabaloo-world full of life
preening itself with its own spirit visible
   like the sheen on a bird's plumage
     everywhere singing
its joys, descending melancholies,
quacks and chorus and calm silence of noon?

White Heron,
   solitary
entering new territory
   wings open
            wings open....
All the rest is unknown,
into it we grow—
            heart open...

   all the wings fluttering
forest full of white wings
     garza blanca gathering

Tiger Heron,
   where the salt water
     meets the sweet—
Green Heron fishing
in the estuary
     cool and deep—
   Blue Heron
     flew over, three times
       in three days
   What does he say?
   Trust your own way.

   white heron, solitary
entering new territory
     wings open

Once there was a great party
and all of us were invited—
rivers and streams, the city people and
wanderers, and all the animals…the party
   was in a circle of trees,
which represented the rest who were
unable to come.
Rocks and sand formed the way,
   and the moon illuminated it.

by canoe, nearing home

in went hands and fingers,
grateful like thirsty animals,
in went cups and bowls
to scoop and bring to mouths,
poured over heads and faces—
   hats dipped in and put back
     on heads—
cool sweet water.
Aucayacu,
   'native waters,'
that's what it means.

Listen, and you will hear its blessed swell
the inside of my ear's a shell
the shape of South America.

This Fish

This
is the last
thing I'll eat
today, this fish
cooked just right
spiced with plants
to eat with a river
view. This nice boy
who serves me asks
would you like to go
to Wasp Lake later?
first, I said, I have
to go home, to
write about this
this
fish.

As the riverboat *Sofy* stopped at one place
along the Ucayali, we watched a scene un-
fold which became trance-like, undulating —
it was near sunset and the colors were
dripping into the waves along the shore,
           swells made by the boat.
The nearby grass was as rich and green
as green could be, with small groups of
children singing laughing scurrying
and finally throwing little bags of water
up onto the deck where we stood,
making passengers squeal and rush back.

  Down below along the shore, a few dugout
canoes moved slowly about. People did a
bit of wash or collected water, and in the
reflective swells between the grasses were
the dark heads and splashing and the joyful
cries of bathers. All was moving between
earth water and sky and the feeling made
people say 'how beautiful'. *'Como un vestido'*
said one man, looking down. 'Like a dress.'
A dress?

  Yes, we can see what you mean, a
fluttering swirl which floats dancing on a
body. A beautiful dress. This place of
riverine life, a place with a pretty name…
what was it? *Sapuena*.
'It makes you see how important water is,'
my daughter said.
'It makes people happy.'

Before stars,
   before honeycomb
before water flowed freely
before the plant grew in the earth
   before the seed—before the cloud
     became a bird, before birth
there was
the beginning of pattern.
It was still an impulse,
   a suggestion, but then
it started to feel...
     is it yet real?
Is it a woman? or statue on a base—
is it water or just design—is it
cloud, or bird?
Are they stars?

plop! go the fruits
     into the water,
   up from beneath
swim the fruit-eaters.

I release into this river of rain
    all sorrow and
    pain....

Water
   rushing, careening
     through chasms
washing, wetting, pulling
   sediments and sentiments
       and song....

I drink
to thank the coming
  of the day

I drink, possessed
as anything
that's free —
to dance
and then to rest
  is sanctity

...And the little madame
   Butterfly
      reached way high up
   and flew higher
     to get all those
   blues from the sky —
those Demetrius blues,
   and she
   dropped them down into
   the sea,
     thinking it was
a good place to store them.

AFTERWORD

ON A WINTER DAY, with snow gently falling, I wrap up this work so that it can be an offering and opening, to you. If it is a large collection that's because I began writing at a young age. I have not tried to include all, but to illustrate a few common themes. Water seems to run through. I have lived in cities and woods, on diverse continents, and often near rivers—which might be why the book took its name. Many experiences reminded me of a childhood vision which I had always known as 'Genesee.' Later I found out it means 'Beautiful River Valley.' I heard the name for the first time when I was ten, while lying on top of an enormous rock, eyes closed, on a hot summer day. In the coolness of a breeze I saw a little river and a canoe gliding downstream. Someone was standing in it. He—or was it she?—was dressed in pale buckskin. 'Genesee' took some crystals out from a pouch and held each one to his third eye; as he went by he tossed them gently to the people who stood along the banks among the green growing things. To me the vision is about renewal, clear water and ongoing life.

This work is a collaboration with Terrence Chouinard, book designer, whose expertise I am most grateful for, in helping to see me through, and this book to print.

FIRST LINES & TITLES

A bird flew by, *20*
A Chrysalis needs *53*
Adventure-giver, Quiverer — at twilight *30*
A frozen spider creeps *71*
Along the ragged oaks *82*
America is dying, and is being born. *39*
And the little madame Butterfly *108*
Anger prodded me *7*
Apu, they call *38*
As the riverboat Sofy stopped at one place *105*
As the steward of my life — *29*
At first it was a whiff of hope *34*
At the princess fountain of the *2*

Before stars, *106*
Big Indian Rock *51*
Blessings on the work *79*
BLUEBERRIES *88*
by canoe, nearing home *102*

CANYON *78*
Celebrate *70*
Chapter 2 — Gradual Development *25*
Colorful—Overeaten *89*
Come, architects — *35*

Dear women and men, *31*

EARLY SPRING *82*
Every last blooming flower *42*
Everywhere, in the bus, the hotel *4*
Every word seems to have its opposite *43*

FIELD DAY 94
Fire, Fire 54
FROG KING 24

GEOMETRY 32
Gone are the honey-solemn songs 16
Green grasses share their dances 17

Happyness, happiness, 74
He laid some giant leaves upon a fallen tree, 98

I AM AMERICA, BLOOMING (TEXAS, 1972) 39
I am a player 12
I barely know where to start, 44
I can tell I have grown, because 15
I don't think I can perceive 21
I dreamed of a sphere, living and precious, 57
I dreamt of a man called Po-Po, intellectual, distinguished, tall— 56
I go to the place of 18
I go wild in the blueberry patch, 88
I had to have a ceremony 81
I have a shell in an upstairs room 14
In the end of human history 64
I put my feet 85
I said it would be 61
I see the Sun 40
I shake my shaggy behind, 68
Is it possible to draw vitality 99
I told my parents, when I grow up 9
I too was once in jail—glad to be released 47
It sometimes felt I got 10
I went to the city for pleasure, 66

Kite field, Judy's field, zig-zag field— 94

Law of life—isn't it funny to think 26
Life—so fragile 96
Listen, and you will hear its blessed swell 103
Little starship in the clearing 59

Many men want to control 6
MEADOW AT NIGHT 49
Milky dove, 95
MOTHER'S DAY 84
My love is a nocturnal hunter 91
my mother ever fertile 65

NEW BEGINNINGS 61
no-one talks about that God, the one 62

Once, ages ago, a sweet goddess-like maid 45
Once there was a great party 101

Rhythms stayed in me from the 48

SELF-CARE 99
Sight comes out of mist 86
Simple I am, Genesee— 52
SNAKE 66
SOLIDAGO 11
Solitude with my allied spirits 27
So now in this brazen autumn 36
Standing in a torrent 73
Stormy and wonderful night— 24

Thank you, grandmother Sun 3
The canyon is the place 78
The cave of my heart says 'Beware', 46
The cows were quiet once the stars came. 49
the earth's my muse and mother, 58
The last Incan Emperor 90
The mother, my mother— 84
THE MOUNDBUILDER 45
THE OLD MERMAID 30
The old worn skin's grown dull, inhibiting. 92
There is a delicacy about the Spring here, 83
there's Goldenrod's face 11
These are the days of weeding and pruning 8
The snake swung down—a half moon hung 55
The sun's a wastrel, 50
The turning— 28
The Word of God is a golden thread, 80
The world makes you 33
This Fish 104
Through the vesica of my eye, the 32
To break away from oppression 23
To integrate self-knowledge 72
trust your sympathies, trust 69

UNDERWORLD 21

VER SACRUM 81

Was it by negligence? obliviousness? 76
Water 107
When a bird trills its song, the surface 97

When I went to the bathroom, moonlight   19
White Heron,   100
WISH   22

You know how the ladybug's wings   5
You must go at once   77
You should not bruise it with your hope,   22

PAMELA LIVINGSTON is a poet, artist and musician who lives in Cherry Valley, New York. *Songs of Genesee* is her first published work.

www.ingramcontent.com/pod-product-compliance
Lightning Source LLC
Chambersburg PA
CBHW030450010526
44118CB00011B/864